CONTENTS

CONTENTS

THOMAS STEARNS ELIOT (1888–1965) was born and raised in St. Louis and studied at Harvard, the Sorbonne, and Oxford before settling in London in 1914 and going on to become one of the most revolutionary poets of the twentieth century. His style marked a radical departure from the form and subject matter of pre–World War I poetry, and both his poetry and literary criticism redefined modern literature. *The Waste Land*, published in 1922, presents a stark metaphor of modern culture and is considered a central masterpiece of the twentieth century. In 1927 Eliot obtained British citizenship. He received the Nobel Prize for Literature in 1948.

HELEN VENDLER is A. Kingsley Porter University Professor at Harvard University. She is a literary critic who has published books on W. B. Yeats, Wallace Stevens, John Keats, and George Herbert, and is also the author of *The Art of Shakespeare's Sonnets*. Vendler writes regularly for *The New Yorker*, *The New York Review of Books*, *The New Republic*, and *London Review of Books*.

T. S. ELIOT

THE WASTE LAND
AND OTHER POEMS

Selected and with
an Introduction by
HELEN VENDLER

A SIGNET CLASSIC

SIGNET CLASSIC
Published by New American Library, a division of
Penguin Group (USA) Inc., 375 Hudson Street,
New York, New York 10014, USA
Penguin Group (Canada), 90 Eglinton Avenue East, Suite 700, Toronto,
Ontario M4P 2Y3, Canada (a division of Pearson Penguin Canada Inc.)
Penguin Books Ltd., 80 Strand, London WC2R 0RL, England
Penguin Ireland, 25 St. Stephen's Green, Dublin 2,
Ireland (a division of Penguin Books Ltd.)
Penguin Group (Australia), 250 Camberwell Road, Camberwell, Victoria 3124,
Australia (a division of Pearson Australia Group Pty. Ltd.)
Penguin Books India Pvt. Ltd., 11 Community Centre, Panchsheel Park,
New Delhi - 110 017, India
Penguin Group (NZ), cnr Airborne and Rosedale Roads, Albany,
Auckland 1310, New Zealand (a division of Pearson New Zealand Ltd.)
Penguin Books (South Africa) (Pty.) Ltd., 24 Sturdee Avenue,
Rosebank, Johannesburg 2196, South Africa

Penguin Books Ltd., Registered Offices:
80 Strand, London WC2R 0RL, England

Published by Signet Classic, an imprint of New American Library,
a division of Penguin Group (USA) Inc.

First Signet Classic Printing, February 1998
30 29 28 27 26

 REGISTERED TRADEMARK—MARCA REGISTRADA

Library of Congress Catalog Card Number: 97-61987

Printed in the United States of America

INTRODUCTION

by Helen Vendler

He is haunted by a demon, a demon against which
he feels powerless, because in its first manifestation
it has no face, no name, nothing; and the words, the
poem he makes, are a kind of form of exorcism of
this demon.
                    —"The Three Voices of Poetry" (1953)[1]

"I can only repeat, but with the urgency of 50 years
ago: READ HIM." Ezra Pound's remark on T. S. Eliot's
death[2] is the implicit message of the countless books
and articles about Eliot issued since the publication of
Prufrock and Other Observations (1917). Eliot has at-
tained the status of a classic—that is, an author who
offers something to everyone. Because philosophical,
religious, political, and poetic interests met in him, his
supreme achievement—the poetry—is often lost sight
of in the disputes concerning his place in international
Modernism, his political affiliations, or his intellectual

development. In the long run, the poetry will last, and the more topical interests will wither. This selection represents the essential Eliot: the poet who, at twenty-six, wrote to Conrad Aiken, "It's interesting to cut yourself to pieces once in a while, and wait to see if the fragments will sprout."[3]

> There I saw one I knew, and stopped him, crying: "Stetson!
> "You who were with me in the ships at Mylae!
> "That corpse you planted last year in your garden,
> "Has it begun to sprout?"
>
> (The Waste Land)

One could think of Eliot's lyrics as amputated bits of the self, temporarily buried, which sprouted into aesthetic form.

The more famous poems of T. S. Eliot have already left behind well-known memory tracks: their famous tag lines

> April is the cruelest month (The Waste Land)

> I grow old . . . I grow old,
> I shall wear the bottoms of my trousers rolled
> ("The Love Song of J. Alfred Prufrock")

> We are the hollow men ("The Hollow Men")

have come to stand for the whole of the poems in which they appear, and those poems—even to Eliot's severest critics—simply remain unforgettable. Eliot put his mark on poetry in the two ways characteristic of the greatest authors: he imposed his imagination of the world on others; and he became indistinguishable from his style. That imagination, and that style, issued from a mind and heart that were passionate, complex, and riven.

Eliot grew up deeply in conflict with himself: repelled by his own fascination with sexual cruelty and his Brahmin sense of innate superiority, he set himself to representing these obsessions while condemning them. He developed into a lacerating ironist of his own emotions ("Prufrock"), and a biting satirist of the social scene ("Whispers of Immortality"); but when he dropped his defenses and gazed into the agony of his own sexuality and sensibility, he composed—with a concentration he could never again duplicate—*The Waste Land*. "These fragments," the poem concludes, "I have shored against my ruins." The "fragments" were bits and pieces of Western and Eastern culture, and the "shoring" was a form of collage (from the French *coller*, "to glue together"): Eliot made a collage, shockingly transitionless, between cultural fragments and scenes both historical and contemporary. He put together *The Waste Land* in the polyglot environment of a Swiss sanitarium where he was recuperating from a nervous breakdown; this may account in part for its polyphonic and multi-tongued music.

The poem longs not only for an inner self Eliot could contemplate without condemnation but also for its corresponding social context, Augustine's City of God (sought among the ruins of postwar Europe, when everyone knew that it was only a matter of time until a second war, revenging the land distribution of the Treaty of Versailles, would break out). Eliot's quest ends in a desert, but with a hope symbolized by "a damp gust / Bringing rain." Under the guidance of three ethical commandments from Buddhism— "give," "sympathize," "control"—the poet hopes for a changed condition, in himself and the world. (These nondoctrinal, broadly ethical commandments lack an institution in which to be socially embodied; and Eliot's later conversion to Anglo-Catholicism—the church officially "established" by the British state— revealed his disillusion with a purely personal ethical system as a means of reforming both self and world.)

The Waste Land—with its new music, its juxtaposition of high and low culture, and its daunting recourse to Latin, Greek, Sanskrit, German, and French (languages completely internalized by, and natural to, Eliot the scholar)—set a new direction for modern poetry and made other poets sit up and take notice. "About enough, Eliot's poem, to make the rest of us shut up shop," wrote Ezra Pound to John Quinn.[4] The reception of the poem varied from conviction that it was a hoax to belief that it was a masterpiece. Though (as we know from the drafts of the poem published by Valerie Eliot) *The Waste Land* originally contained scenes set in Boston and Gloucester, in the revision all American references were cut. The modernist Euro-poem had been born.

It was a very learned but hitherto inconspicuous poet who published *The Waste Land*. Eliot, the young-est of seven children, was born in 1888 in St. Louis to a well-off family of displaced New Englanders: his father (Henry Ware Eliot) headed a company that manufactured bricks, his mother (Charlotte Stearns Champe Eliot) was a former schoolteacher. The poet's ancestor Andrew Eliot had arrived in New England in the seventeenth century, and the family, originally Calvinist, had declined, by the time Eliot was born, into a genteel Unitarianism. Eliot's mother was herself a poet, and critics have remarked on the parallels be-tween her religious interests and those of her son: but while her poetry is untroubled in its devotion, his was never less than tormented by philosophical skepticism on the one hand and fear of personal damnation on the other.

At seventeen Eliot entered Harvard, where he re-mained a brilliant student until he was about to com-plete a Ph.D. in philosophy. But he had been writing poetry since his senior year in college, and study in France after he graduated had made Europe tempting to him. When he left his graduate program at Harvard for a year of study at Oxford, everyone (including a young New England woman named Emily Hale, to whom he was deeply drawn, and to whom he wrote some one thousand letters over his lifetime) expected him to return with his dissertation completed and to become an instructor in philosophy at Harvard. Though Eliot finished the dissertation, he never returned from England. In London, he had come to know Ezra Pound and had decided for the life of poetry; he had also met, and married on impulse, a young Englishwoman named Vivien Haigh-Wood. (Their childless marriage [1915–33], plagued by her desperate sicknesses—colitis, migraines, rheumatism, hormonal irregularities, and "nerves" for which there were then no satisfactory remedies—and by the poet's eventual nervous breakdown in 1921, was deeply unhappy, and ended in a formal separation initiated by Eliot; Vivien died in 1947 in a mental institution to which she had been confined for seven years.)

In 1917, after a brief spell of teaching, Eliot found employment at Lloyd's Bank in London, work from which he was relieved when he became a member, from 1925 till the end of his life, of the board of directors of the publishers Faber and Gwyer (later Faber and Faber). It was in 1917 that he published *Prufrock and Other Observations*; between that time and 1921 he was composing the separate poems which, cut and collaged with the editorial help of Ezra Pound, made up *The Waste Land* (1922). Between these volumes Eliot had established himself, with the essays collected in *The Sacred Wood* (1920), as a revolutionary critic of poetry, emphasizing—against those who considered poetry merely an outpouring of emotion—the aesthetic impersonality of a work of art: "The progress of an artist is a continual self-sacrifice, a continual extinction of personality."[5] And, as editor of *The Criterion* (1922–39), he became a powerful force in shaping literary and intellectual taste. In 1927 Eliot formally converted to Anglo-Catholicism, and became a British citizen. In 1932 he published (in fragmentary form) his first play, *Sweeney Agonistes*. In 1942 he wrote his last significant poem, "Little Gidding." In 1948 Eliot was awarded the Nobel Prize; in 1957, at sixty-eight, he married his young secretary Valerie Fletcher; in 1965 he died.

The public Eliot—hardworking editor at Faber, genial benefactor of young writers—concealed a man whose inner sufferings can be gauged only through his poetry, which conceals nothing. Most poets (though not all) have thought *The Waste Land* to be the high point of Eliot's poetic invention, and poets tend to be good judges of their predecessors. But poets judge principally by aesthetic criteria: "Has the imagination succeeded in finding a symbolic equivalent for its emotional predicament? Has a new lyric structure been invented, as passion struggles to embody itself in form? Is the voice memorable, the language original? Has the presented emotional situation created its own complex of aesthetic feeling?" Some readers (mostly those who are not poets) have felt, chiefly on the basis of Eliot's struggle toward spirituality, that his last poems (written between 1935 and 1942), which he called Quartets after the musical example, are more admirable, more ethically and philosophically mature, than *The Waste Land*. The chaste, consistent, and abstract style of the Quartets seems to them preferable to the welter of names, languages, and styles in *The Waste Land*. Whatever one's judgement of relative worth, it is historically undeniable that the early poems—those in this selection—were the ones that revolutionized poetic practice in the twentieth century, not only by their skepticism and despair over the nature of modernity, and not only by the picture they gave of an alienated and fastidious mind renewing the lyric genres, but also by their opposing poles of prosody: satiric strict quantrains, dryly metaphysical, in some poems, and in others, a haunting free-verse rhythm always approaching regular meter, then withdrawing from it.

After composing the Quartets, Eliot ceased to be a lyric poet: the tense psychological conflicts that had fed the lyrics could find no new style, no new lyric rhythm. Eliot abhorred the idea of repeating himself, and the sort of passion that forces a change of voice (as in the turn from "Preludes" to *The Waste Land*, or from *The Waste Land* to the Quartets) was, in his later life, either absent, or too greatly diminished in strength to carve a further channel. He died as a lyric poet in 1942 (when he composed the last Quartet, "Little Gidding") but endured, before his actual death in 1965, two decades of "posthumous" existence—as dramatist, essayist, comic poet ("Old Possum's Book of Practical Cats"), editor, and elder statesman of letters. It is ironic that his principal claim to popular fame should be the musical *Cats*, drawn from his least serious verse.

I have called Eliot's later life a posthumous existence because, for all the energy of his polemic prose, and for all the seriousness of his plays, it is as a lyric poet that Eliot discovered his radical style of free verse and changed the face of modern literature. His verse dramas show no sign of holding the stage (any more than those of Wordsworth, Coleridge, Shelley, or Tennyson); and the cultural issues addressed by his prose, while perennial ones, have shifted intellectual ground. Of the prose works, the essays on poetry have proved most lasting: although Eliot's underlying biases (in favor of the complex, the philosophical, and the religious in poetry) are undeniable, his intelligence and learning, his subtlety of appreciation, his eye for the telling piece of evidence, and his genius for describing poetic effects remain unmatched among modern essayists. His writings on poetry are, naturally enough, disguised manifestos for his own practice, but that is always the case with poets: they work out their own theory through commenting on the practice of their predecessors. Although it is still exhilarating to discover Eliot on Dante or on Donne, on tradition or criticism, to read his poetry is to be changed in one's own being.

What was Eliot's conception of the act of writing poetry? In a 1939 essay entitled "That Poetry Is Made with Words," he wrote:

> Poetry, if it is not to be a lifeless repetition of forms, must be constantly exploring "the frontiers of the spirit." But these frontiers are not like the surveys of geographical explorers, conquered once for all and settled. The frontiers of the spirit are more like the jungle which, unless continuously kept under control, is always ready to encroach and eventually obliterate the cultivated area.[6]

That "jungle" is the jungle of the emotions, constantly changing under changing historical conditions, so that the modern poet wishing to understand and represent the present must be in constant dialogue with human experience recorded in the past:

> Emotions themselves are constantly being lost; they can never be merely preserved, but must be always re-discovered. . . . Just as history has constantly to be re-written, because everything is gradually altered by the lengthening perspective; so also the poet needs an alert conscious-

ness of the past, in order to realise in its particular concreteness the moment at which he lives.[7]

Eliot adds, though, that the first responsibility of the poet (by contrast to the person who thinks and feels but does not write) is to language:

> A ceaseless care, a passionate and untiring devotion to language, is the first conscious concern of the poet; it demands study of how his language has been written, in both prose and verse, in the past, and sensitiveness to the merits and shortcomings of the way in which it is spoken and written in his own time.[8]

Eliot prepared himself for writing poetry by omnivorously ingesting the past of the English language from Chaucer through Tennyson; and he investigated its present state not only in literature but in pub and music hall, church and theater. His preternaturally acute sense of spoken English (sound, intonation, and rhythm) was intensified by his study of classical, Indic, and modern foreign languages; and his aesthetic claim on our attention (like that of Joyce) is exerted in the first instance by the sheer breadth and variety of his linguistic and vocal repertoire. There is the jazz Eliot, the allegorical Eliot, the music hall Eliot, the learned Eliot, the mystical Eliot, the philosophical Eliot. There is surprise in every stanza of Eliot—it is impossible to forecast where his incomparable voice will go. Yet there is purposefulness in its wandering: as the poem completes itself linearly, it also takes on a crystalline spatial structure that replicates, in its textual feeling, a pattern of human emotion.

Eliot formulated what the whole poem should be in "The Love Song of J. Alfred Prufrock," the poem in which he exultantly discovered how to represent his emotions without being mastered by them. In "Prufrock's Pervigilium" (the recently published draft of a part of the poem, subsequently cancelled), he momentarily allowed himself to succumb to his own hysteria listening to his "Madness singing":

> I fumbled to the window to experience the world
> And to hear my Madness singing, sitting on the
>   kerbstone
> [A blind old drunken man who sings and mutters,
> With broken boot heels stained in many gutters].[9]

By the time of the completed "Prufrock" the poem had become not an unmediated outburst but an analytic diagnosis in patterned language, or as Eliot put it in a famous modernist simile, "As if a magic lantern threw the nerves in patterns on a screen." There is no more brilliant moment in Eliot's development than the metamorphosis of his "Madness," that "blind old drunken man who sings," into the mermaids:

> I have heard the mermaids singing, each to each.

Eliot can hear the mermaid-Muses, however intermittently, only when he has thrown the convulsions of his "nerves," his "madness," in formal patterns on the aesthetic screen of the text. To make the effort of compositional detachment—to look at one's Madness from outside one's Madness, to perceive his characterizing patterns, and to find a screen on which to throw them—is the task demanded of the poet. When Eliot saw this and was able to do it by means of ineffaceable language, he became the writer it was in him to be. The world noticed this rare achievement, as it always will. There are only a few persons in any generation who can make inner human emotions visible in a rhythmic linguistic structure bearing aesthetic feeling, conveying, in a transhistorical way, the sensation of being alive at a particular historical period. We call such persons poets: in becoming such a person, Eliot became a crystallizer of emotional response for his whole epoch.

NOTES

1. *On Poetry and Poets* (London: Faber and Faber, 1957), p. 98.

2. Ezra Pound, "For T. S. E.," *Sewanee Review* 74 (January–March 1966): 109.

3. *The Letters of T. S. Eliot*, Volume I: 1898–1922, ed. Valerie Eliot (Harcourt Brace, 1988), p. 59.

4. Ezra Pound to John Quinn, letter of 21 February 1922.

5. *The Sacred Wood: Essays on Poetry and Criticism* (London: Methuen, 1920; rpt. New York: Barnes and Noble, 1966), p. 53.

6. *New English Weekly* 15 (27 April 1939): 27.

7. Ibid.

8. Ibid., 28.

9. *Inventions of the March Hare*, ed. Christopher Ricks (New York: Harcourt Brace, 1997), p. 43.

THE WASTE LAND
AND OTHER POEMS

———

SPLEEN[1]

Sunday: this satisfied procession
Of definite Sunday faces;
Bonnets, silk hats, and conscious graces
In repetition that displaces
Your mental self-possession   5
By this unwarranted digression.

Evening, lights, and tea!
Children and cats in the alley;
Dejection unable to rally
Against this dull conspiracy.   10

And Life, a little bald and gray,
Languid, fastidious, and bland,
Waits, hat and gloves in hand,
Punctilious of tie and suit
(Somewhat impatient of delay)   15
   On the doorstep of the Absolute.

                                        (1910)

THE DEATH OF SAINT NARCISSUS[1]

––––––––

Come under the shadow of this gray rock—
Come in under the shadow of this gray rock,
And I will show you something different from either
Your shadow sprawling over the sand at daybreak,

or

Your shadow leaping behind the fire against the red

rock: 5

I will show you his bloody cloth and limbs
And the gray shadow on his lips.

He walked once between the sea and the high cliffs
When the wind made him aware of his limbs

smoothly passing each other

And of his arms crossed over his breast. 10
When he walked over the meadows
He was stifled and soothed by his own rhythm.
By the river
His eyes were aware of the pointed corners of his

eyes

And his hands aware of the pointed tips of his
                                    fingers.   15
Struck down by such knowledge
He could not live men's ways, but became a dancer
                                    before God
If he walked in city streets
He seemed to tread on faces, convulsive thighs and
                                    knees.
So he came out under the rock.   20

    First he was sure that he had been a tree,[2]
Twisting its branches among each other
And tangling its roots among each other.

    Then he knew that he had been a fish
With slippery white belly held tight in his own
                                    fingers,   25
Writhing in his own clutch, his ancient beauty
Caught fast in the pink tips of his new beauty.

    Then he had been a young girl
Caught in the woods by a drunken old man
Knowing at the end the taste of his own whiteness   30
The horror of his own smoothness,
And he felt drunken and old.

    So he became a dancer to God.
Because his flesh was in love with the burning
                                    arrows
He danced on the hot sand   35

Until the arrows came.
As he embraced them his white skin surrendered
                                    itself to the redness of
                                blood, and satisfied him.
Now he is green, dry and stained
With the shadow in his mouth.   40

(Unknown date—from galley proof of
Poetry [Chicago], probably between
1910 and 1915)

THE LOVE SONG OF J. ALFRED PRUFROCK

S'io credesse che mia risposta fosse
A persona che mai tornasse al mondo,
Questa fiamma staria senza piu scosse.
Ma perciocche giammai di questo fondo
Non torno vivo alcun, s'i'odo il vero,
Senza tema d'infamia ti rispondo.[1]

Let us go then, you and I,
When the evening is spread out against the sky
Like a patient etherised upon a table;
Let us go, through certain half-deserted streets,
The muttering retreats   5
Of restless nights in one-night cheap hotels
And sawdust restaurants with oyster-shells:
Streets that follow like a tedious argument
Of insidious intent
To lead you to an overwhelming question . . .   10

Oh, do not ask, "What is it?"
Let us go and make our visit.

In the room the women come and go
Talking of Michelangelo.

The yellow fog that rubs its back upon the
window-panes, 15
The yellow smoke that rubs its muzzle on the
window-panes
Licked its tongue into the corners of the evening,
Lingered upon the pools that stand in drains,
Let fall upon its back the soot that falls from
chimneys,
Slipped by the terrace, made a sudden leap,   20
And seeing that it was a soft October night,
Curled once about the house, and fell asleep.

And indeed there will be time
For the yellow smoke that slides along the street,
Rubbing its back upon the window-panes;   25
There will be time, there will be time
To prepare a face to meet the faces that you meet;
There will be time to murder and create.
And time for all the works and days² of hands
That lift and drop a question on your plate;   30
Time for you and time for me,
And time yet for a hundred indecisions,

And for a hundred visions and revisions,
Before the taking of a toast and tea.

   In the room the women come and go   36
Talking of Michelangelo.

   And indeed there will be time
To wonder, "Do I dare?" and, "Do I dare?"
Time to turn back and descend the stair,
With a bald spot in the middle of my hair—   40
[They will say: "How his hair is growing thin!"]
My morning coat, my collar mounting firmly to the
                                   chin,
My necktie rich and modest, but asserted by a simple
                                   pin—
[They will say: "But how his arms and legs are
                                   thin!"]
Do I dare   45
Disturb the universe?
In a minute there is time
For decisions and revisions which a minute will
                                   reverse.

   For I have known them all already, known them
                                   all:—
Have known the evenings, mornings, afternoons,   50
I have measured out my life with coffee spoons;
I know the voices dying with a dying fall

Beneath the music from a farther room.
　So how should I presume?

　And I have known the eyes already, known them
　　　　　　　　　　　　　　　　　　all—　55
The eyes that fix you in a formulated phrase,
And when I am formulated, sprawling on a pin,
When I am pinned and wriggling on the wall,
Then how should I begin
To spit out all the butt-ends of my days and ways?　60
　And how should I presume?

　And I have known the arms already, known them
　　　　　　　　　　　　　　　　　　all—
Arms that are braceleted and white and bare
[But in the lamplight, downed with light brown
　　　　　　　　　　　　　　　　　　hair!]
Is it perfume from a dress　65
That makes me so digress?
Arms that lie along a table, or wrap about a shawl.
　And should I then presume?
　And how should I begin?

　　　　　　. . . . .

Shall I say, I have gone at dusk through narrow
　　　　　　　　　　　　　　　　streets　70
And watched the smoke that rises from the pipes
Of lonely men in shirt-sleeves, leaning out of
　　　　　　　　　　　　　　　windows? . . .

I should have been a pair of ragged claws
Scuttling across the floors of silent seas.

. . . . .

And the afternoon, the evening, sleeps so peacefully!   75
Smoothed by long fingers,
Asleep . . . tired . . . or it malingers,
Stretched on the floor, here beside you and me.
Should I, after tea and cakes and ices,
Have the strength to force the moment to its crisis?   80
But though I have wept and fasted, wept and prayed,
Though I have seen my head [grown slightly bald]
                       brought in upon a platter,[3]
I am no prophet—and here's no great matter;
I have seen the moment of my greatness flicker,
And I have seen the eternal Footman hold my coat,
                       and snicker,   85
And in short, I was afraid.

And would it have been worth it, after all,
After the cups, the marmalade, the tea,
Among the porcelain, among some talk of you and
                              me,
Would it have been worth while,   90
To have bitten off the matter with a smile,
To have squeezed the universe into a ball
To roll it toward some overwhelming question,
To say: "I am Lazarus, come from the dead,[4]

Come back to tell you all, I shall tell you all"— 95
If one, settling a pillow by her head,
    Should say: "That is not what I meant at all.
    That is not it, at all."

    And would it have been worth it, after all,
Would it have been worth while, 100
After the sunsets and the dooryards and the
                                        sprinkled streets,
After the novels, after the teacups, after the skirts that
                                        trail along the floor—
And this, and so much more?—
It is impossible to say just what I mean!
But as if a magic lantern threw the nerves in patterns
                                        on a screen: 105
Would it have been worth while
If one, settling a pillow or throwing off a shawl,
And turning toward the window, should say:
    "That is not it at all,
    That is not what I meant, at all." 110

. . . . .

No! I am not Prince Hamlet,[5] nor was meant to be;
Am an attendant lord, one that will do
To swell a progress,[6] start a scene or two,
Advise the prince; no doubt, an easy tool,
Deferential, glad to be of use, 115
Politic, cautious, and meticulous;

Full of high sentence,[7] but a bit obtuse;
At times, indeed, almost ridiculous—
Almost, at times, the Fool.

I grow old . . . I grow old . . .   120
I shall wear the bottoms of my trousers rolled.

Shall I part my hair behind? Do I dare to eat a
                                    peach?
I shall wear white flannel trousers, and walk upon
                               the beach.
I have heard the mermaids singing, each to each.

I do not think that they will sing to me.   125

I have seen them riding seaward on the waves
Combing the white hair of the waves blown back
When the wind blows the water white and black.

We have lingered in the chambers of the sea
By sea-girls wreathed with seaweed red and brown   130
Till human voices wake us, and we drown.

                                    (1917)

PRELUDES[1]

———

I

The winter evening settles down
With smell of steaks in passageways.
Six o'clock.
The burnt-out ends of smoky days.
And now a gusty shower wraps   5
The grimy scraps
Of withered leaves about your feet
And newspapers from vacant lots;
The showers beat
On broken blinds and chimney-pots,   10
And at the corner of the street
A lonely cab-horse steams and stamps.
And then the lighting of the lamps.

II

The morning comes to consciousness
Of faint stale smells of beer   15
From the sawdust-trampled street
With all its muddy feet that press
To early coffee-stands.
With the other masquerades
That time resumes,   20
One thinks of all the hands
That are raising dingy shades
In a thousand furnished rooms.

III

You tossed a blanket from the bed,
You lay upon your back, and waited;   25
You dozed, and watched the night revealing
The thousand sordid images
Of which your soul was constituted;
They flickered against the ceiling.
And when all the world came back   30
And the light crept up between the shutters

And you heard the sparrows in the gutters,
You had such a vision of the street
As the street hardly understands;
Sitting along the bed's edge, where   35
You curled the papers from your hair,
Or clasped the yellow soles of feet
In the palms of both soiled hands.

IV

His soul stretched tight across the skies
That fade behind a city block,   40
Or trampled by insistent feet
At four and five and six o'clock;
And short square fingers stuffing pipes,
And evening newspapers, and eyes
Assured of certain certainties,   45
The conscience of a blackened street
Impatient to assume the world.

  I am moved by fancies that are curled
Around these images, and cling:
The notion of some infinitely gentle   50
Infinitely suffering thing.

—

Wipe your hand across your mouth, and laugh;
The worlds revolve like ancient women
Gathering fuel in vacant lots.

(1917)

THE *BOSTON EVENING TRANSCRIPT*[1]

———

The readers of the *Boston Evening Transcript*
Sway in the wind like a field of ripe corn.

  When evening quickens faintly in the street,
Wakening the appetites of life in some
And to others bringing the *Boston Evening Transcript*,   5
I mount the steps and ring the bell, turning
Wearily, as one would turn to nod good-bye to
                          Rochefoucauld,
If the street were time and he at the end of the street,
And I say, "Cousin Harriet, here is the *Boston Evening*
                           Transcript."

                            (1917)

HYSTERIA[1]

As she laughed I was aware of becoming involved in her laughter and being part of it, until her teeth were only accidental stars with a talent for squad-drill. I was drawn in by short gasps, inhaled at each momentary recovery, lost finally in the dark caverns of her throat, bruised by the ripple of unseen muscles. An elderly waiter with trembling hands was hurriedly spreading a pink and white checked cloth over the rusty green iron table, saying: "If the lady and gentleman wish to take their tea in the garden, if the lady and gentleman wish to take their tea in the garden . . ." I decided that if the shaking of her breasts could be stopped, some of the fragments of the afternoon might be collected, and I concentrated my attention with careful subtlety to this end.

(1917)

LA FIGLIA CHE PIANGE[1]

O quam te memorem virgo . . .[2]

Stand on the highest pavement of the stair—
Lean on a garden urn—
Weave, weave the sunlight in your hair—
Clasp your flowers to you with a pained surprise—
Fling them to the ground and turn   5
With a fugitive resentment in your eyes:
But weave, weave the sunlight in your hair.

  So I would have had him leave,
So I would have had her stand and grieve,
So he would have left   10
As the soul leaves the body torn and bruised,
As the mind deserts the body it has used.
I should find
Some way incomparably light and deft,

Some way we both should understand,   15
Simple and faithless as a smile and shake of the
                                        hand.

   She turned away, but with the autumn weather
Compelled my imagination many days,
Many days and many hours:
Her hair over her arms and her arms full of flowers.   20
And I wonder how they should have been together!
I should have lost a gesture and a pose.
Sometimes these cogitations still amaze
The troubled midnight and the noon's repose.

(1917)

GERONTION[1]

Thou hast nor youth nor age
But as it were an after dinner sleep
Dreaming of both.[2]

Here I am, an old man in a dry month,
Being read to by a boy, waiting for rain.
I was neither at the hot gates[3]
Nor fought in the warm rain
Nor knee deep in the salt marsh, heaving a cutlass,   5
Bitten by flies, fought.
My house is a decayed house,
And the jew squats on the window sill, the owner,
Spawned in some estaminet of Antwerp,
Blistered in Brussels, patched and peeled in London.   10
The goat coughs at night in the field overhead;
Rocks, moss, stonecrop, iron, merds.[4]
The woman keeps the kitchen, makes tea,

Sneezes at evening, poking the peevish gutter.

                            I an old man,   15

A dull head among windy spaces.

   Signs are taken for wonders.[5] "We would see a

                                   sign!"

The word within a word, unable to speak a word,

Swaddled with darkness. In the juvescence of the

                                      year

Came Christ the tiger   20

   In depraved May, dogwood and chestnut,

                           flowering judas,

To be eaten, to be divided, to be drunk

Among whispers; by Mr. Silvero

With caressing hands, at Limoges

Who walked all night in the next room;   25

   By Hakagawa, bowing among the Titians;

By Madame de Tornquist, in the dark room

Shifting the candles; Fräulein von Kulp

Who turned in the hall, one hand on the door.

    Vacant shuttles   30

Weave the wind. I have no ghosts,

An old man in a draughty house

Under a windy knob.

   After such knowledge, what forgiveness? Think

                                  now

History has many cunning passages, contrived
corridors 35
And issues, deceives with whispering ambitions,
Guides us by vanities. Think now
She gives when our attention is distracted
And what she gives, gives with such supple
confusions
That the giving famishes the craving. Gives too late 40
What's not believed in, or if still believed,
In memory only, reconsidered passion. Gives too
soon
Into weak hands, what's thought can be dispensed
with
Till the refusal propagates a fear. Think
Neither fear nor courage saves us. Unnatural vices 45
Are fathered by our heroism. Virtues
Are forced upon us by our impudent crimes.
These tears are shaken from the wrath-bearing tree.

The tiger springs in the new year. Us he devours.
Think at last
We have not reached conclusion, when I 50
Stiffen in a rented house. Think at last
I have not made this show purposelessly
And it is not by any concitation
Of the backward devils.
I would meet you upon this honestly. 55
I that was near your heart was removed therefrom

To lose beauty in terror, terror in inquisition.
I have lost my passion: why should I need to keep it
Since what is kept must be adulterated?
I have lost my sight, smell, hearing, taste and touch: 60
How should I use them for your closer contact?

   These with a thousand small deliberations
Protract the profit of their chilled delirium,
Excite the membrane, when the sense has cooled,
With pungent sauces, multiply variety   65
In a wilderness of mirrors. What will the spider do,
Suspend its operations, will the weevil
Delay? De Bailhache, Fresca, Mrs. Cammel, whirled
Beyond the circuit of the shuddering Bear[6]
In fractured atoms. Gull against the wind, in the
                        windy straits   70
Of Belle Isle, or running on the Horn,
White feathers in the snow, the Gulf claims,
And an old man driven by the Trades
To a sleepy corner.[7]

                      Tenants of the house,   75
Thoughts of a dry brain in a dry season.

                           (1920)

THE HIPPOPOTAMUS

Similiter et omnes revereantur Diaconos, ut mandatum Jesu Christi; et Episcopum, ut Jesum Christum, existentem filium Patris; Presbyteros autem, ut concilium Dei et conjunctionem Apostolorum. Sine his Ecclesia non vocatur; de quibus suadeo vos sic habeo.

S. Ignatii Ad Trallianos.[1]

And when this epistle is read among you, cause that it be read also in the church of the Laodiceans.

The broad-backed hippopotamus
Rests on his belly in the mud;
Although he seems so firm to us
He is merely flesh and blood.

Flesh and blood is weak and frail,   5
Susceptible to nervous shock;
While the True Church can never fail
For it is based upon a rock.

The hippo's feeble steps may err
In compassing material ends,   10
While the True Church need never stir
To gather in its dividends.

The 'potamus can never reach
The mango on the mango-tree;
But fruits of pomegranate and peach   15
Refresh the Church from over sea.

At mating time the hippo's voice
Betrays inflexions hoarse and odd,
But every week we hear rejoice
The Church, at being one with God.   20

The hippopotamus's day
Is passed in sleep; at night he hunts;
God works in a mysterious way—
The Church can sleep and feed at once.

I saw the 'potamus take wing   25
Ascending from the damp savannas,
And quiring angels round him sing
The praise of God, in loud hosannas.

Blood of the Lamb shall wash him clean
And him shall heavenly arms enfold,   30
Among the saints he shall be seen
Performing on a harp of gold.

He shall be washed as white as snow,
By all the martyr'd virgins kist,
While the True Church remains below   35
Wrapt in the old miasmal mist.

(1920)

WHISPERS OF IMMORTALITY

Webster[1] was much possessed by death
And saw the skull beneath the skin;
And breastless creatures under ground
Leaned backward with a lipless grin.

    Daffodil bulbs instead of balls   5
Stared from the sockets of the eyes!
He knew that thought clings round dead limbs
Tightening its lusts and luxuries.

    Donne, I suppose, was such another
Who found no substitute for sense,   10
To seize and clutch and penetrate;
Expert beyond experience,

    He knew the anguish of the marrow
The ague of the skeleton;
No contact possible to flesh   15
Allayed the fever of the bone.

. . . . .

Grishkin is nice: her Russian eye
Is underlined for emphasis;
Uncorseted, her friendly bust
Gives promise of pneumatic bliss.   20

　The couched Brazilian jaguar
Compels the scampering marmoset
With subtle effluence of cat;
Grishkin has a maisonette;

　The sleek Brazilian jaguar   25
Does not in its arboreal gloom
Distil so rank a feline smell
As Grishkin in a drawing-room.

　And even the Abstract Entities
Circumambulate her charm;   30
But our lot crawls between dry ribs
To keep our metaphysics warm.

                                        (1920)

SWEENEY AMONG THE NIGHTINGALES

ὤμοι, πέπληγμαι καιρίαν πληγὴν ἔσω.[1]

Apeneck Sweeney[2] spreads his knees
Letting his arms hang down to laugh,
The zebra stripes along his jaw
Swelling to maculate[3] giraffe.

The circles of the stormy moon   5
Slide westward toward the River Plate,[4]
Death and the Raven drift above
And Sweeney guards the hornèd gate.[5]

Gloomy Orion and the Dog[6]
Are veiled; and hushed the shrunken seas;   10
The person in the Spanish cape
Tries to sit on Sweeney's knees

Slips and pulls the table cloth
Overturns a coffee-cup,
Reorganized upon the floor   15
She yawns and draws a stocking up;

The silent man in mocha brown
Sprawls at the window-sill and gapes;
The waiter brings in oranges
Bananas figs and hothouse grapes;   20

The silent vertebrate in brown
Contracts and concentrates, withdraws;
Rachel *née* Rabinovitch
Tears at the grapes with murderous paws;

She and the lady in the cape   25
Are suspect, thought to be in league;
Therefore the man with heavy eyes
Declines the gambit, shows fatigue,

Leaves the room and reappears
Outside the window, leaning in,   30
Branches of wistaria
Circumscribe a golden grin;

The host with someone indistinct
Converses at the door apart,
The nightingales are singing near   35
The Convent of the Sacred Heart,

And sang within the bloody wood
When Agamemnon cried aloud,
And let their liquid siftings fall
To stain the stiff dishonoured shroud.   40

(1920)

THE WASTE LAND*

"Nam Sibyllam quidem Cumis ego ipse oculis meis vidi in ampulla pendere, et cum illi pueri dicerent: Σίβυλλα τί θέλεις; respondebat illa: ἀποθανεῖν θέλω."[1]

For Ezra Pound
il miglior fabbro.[2]

I.
THE BURIAL OF THE DEAD[3]

April is the cruellest month, breeding
Lilacs out of the dead land, mixing
Memory and desire, stirring

*Eliot's notes are printed after the text of the poem. His notes are referred to in parentheses in the endnotes of this edition by E followed by the section number of the poem in roman numerals and the line number in arabic, e.g., (E.,II,32).

Dull roots with spring rain.
Winter kept us warm, covering   5
Earth in forgetful snow, feeding
A little life with dried tubers.
Summer surprised us, coming over the
                              Starnbergersee[4]
With a shower of rain; we stopped in the colonnade,
And went on in sunlight, into the Hofgarten,[5]   10
And drank coffee, and talked for an hour.
Bin gar keine Russin, stamm' aus Litauen, echt
                              deutsch.[6]
And when we were children, staying at the
                              archduke's,
My cousin's, he took me out on a sled,
And I was frightened. He said, Marie,   15
Marie, hold on tight. And down we went.
In the mountains, there you feel free.
I read, much of the night, and go south in the winter.

   What are the roots that clutch, what branches grow
Out of this stony rubbish? Son of man,[7]   20
You cannot say, or guess, for you know only
A heap of broken images, where the sun beats,
And the dead tree gives no shelter, the cricket no
                              relief,[8]
And the dry stone no sound of water. Only
There is shadow under this red rock,   25
(Come in under the shadow of this red rock),[9]

And I will show you something different from either
Your shadow at morning striding behind you
Or your shadow at evening rising to meet you;
I will show you fear in a handful of dust.[10]   30

> *Frisch weht der Wind*
> *Der Heimat zu*
> *Mein Irisch Kind,*
> *Wo weilest du?*[11]

"You gave me hyacinths first a year ago;   35
"They called me the hyacinth girl."
—Yet when we came back, late, from the Hyacinth
                                                        garden,
Your arms full, and your hair wet, I could not
Speak, and my eyes failed, I was neither
Living nor dead, and I knew nothing,   40
Looking into the heart of light, the silence.
Oed' und leer das Meer.[12]

  Madame Sosostris, famous clairvoyante,
Had a bad cold, nevertheless
Is known to be the wisest woman in Europe,   45
With a wicked pack of cards.[13] Here, said she,
Is your card, the drowned Phoenician Sailor,
(Those are pearls that were his eyes.[14] Look!)
Here is Belladonna, the Lady of the Rocks,
The lady of situations.   50
Here is the man with three staves, and here the
                                                        Wheel,

And here is the one-eyed merchant, and this card,
Which is blank, is something he carries on his back,
Which I am forbidden to see. I do not find
The Hanged Man. Fear death by water.   55
I see crowds of people, walking round in a ring.
Thank you. If you see dear Mrs. Equitone,
Tell her I bring the horoscope myself:
One must be so careful these days.

    Unreal City,   60
Under the brown fog of a winter dawn,
A crowd flowed over London Bridge, so many,
I had not thought death had undone so many.[15]
Sighs, short and infrequent, were exhaled,
And each man fixed his eyes before his feet.   65
Flowed up the hill and down King William Street,
To where Saint Mary Woolnoth[16] kept the hours
With a dead sound on the final stroke of nine.
There I saw one I knew, and stopped him, crying:
                                    "Stetson!
"You who were with me in the ships at Mylae![17]   70
"That corpse you planted last year in your garden,
"Has it begun to sprout? Will it bloom this year?
"Or has the sudden frost disturbed its bed?
"Oh keep the Dog far hence, that's friend to men,
"Or with his nails he'll dig it up again![18]   75
"You! hypocrite lecteur!—mon semblable,—mon
                                    frère!"[19]

II.
A GAME OF CHESS[20]

The Chair she sat in, like a burnished throne,
Glowed on the marble,[21] where the glass
Held up by standards wrought with fruited vines
From which a golden Cupidon[22] peeped out   80
(Another hid his eyes behind his wing)
Doubled the flames of sevenbranched candelabra
Reflecting light upon the table as
The glitter of her jewels rose to meet it,
From satin cases poured in rich profusion;   85
In vials of ivory and coloured glass
Unstoppered, lurked her strange synthetic perfumes,
Unguent, powdered, or liquid—troubled, confused
And drowned the sense in odours; stirred by the air
That freshened from the window, these ascended   90
In fattening the prolonged candle-flames,
Flung their smoke into the laquearia,[23]
Stirring the pattern on the coffered ceiling.
Huge sea-wood fed with copper
Burned green and orange, framed by the coloured
                                           stone,   95
In which sad light a carvèd dolphin swam.
Above the antique mantel was displayed
As though a window gave upon the sylvan scene[24]

The change of Philomel,[25] by the barbarous king
So rudely forced; yet there the nightingale   100
Filled all the desert with inviolable voice
And still she cried, and still the world pursues,
"Jug Jug"[26] to dirty ears.
And other withered stumps of time
Were told upon the walls; staring forms   105
Leaned out, leaning, hushing the room enclosed.
Footsteps shuffled on the stair.
Under the firelight, under the brush, her hair
Spread out in fiery points
Glowed into words, then would be savagely still.   110

   "My nerves are bad to-night. Yes, bad. Stay with
                            me.
"Speak to me. Why do you never speak. Speak.
   "What are you thinking of? What thinking? What?
"I never know what you are thinking. Think."

   I think we are in rats' alley   115
Where the dead men lost their bones.

   "What is that noise?"
                  The wind under the door.
"What is that noise now? What is the wind doing?"
                Nothing again nothing.   120
                        "Do
"You know nothing? Do you see nothing? Do you
                        remember
"Nothing?"

I remember
Those are pearls that were his eyes.   125
"Are you alive, or not? Is there nothing in your
                                              head?"
                                                    But

O O O O that Shakespeherian Rag—
It's so elegant
So intelligent[27]   130
"What shall I do now? What shall I do?"
"I shall rush out as I am, and walk the street
"With my hair down, so. What shall we do
                                          to-morrow?
"What shall we ever do?"
                              The hot water at ten.   135
And if it rains, a closed car at four.
And we shall play a game of chess,
Pressing lidless eyes and waiting for a knock upon
                                              the door.

    When Lil's husband got demobbed,[28] I said—
I didn't mince my words, I said to her myself,   140
HURRY UP PLEASE ITS TIME[29]
Now Albert's coming back, make yourself a bit
                                              smart.
He'll want to know what you done with that money
                                        he gave you

To get yourself some teeth. He did, I was there.
You have them all out, Lil, and get a nice set,.   145
He said, I swear, I can't bear to look at you.
And no more can't I, I said, and think of poor Albert,
He's been in the army four years, he wants a good
                                                    time,
And if you don't give it him, there's others will, I
                                                    said.
Oh is there, she said. Something o' that, I said.   150
Then I'll know who to thank, she said, and give me
                                        a straight look.

HURRY UP PLEASE ITS TIME
If you don't like it you can get on with it, I said.
Others can pick and choose if you can't.
But if Albert makes off, it won't be for lack of telling. 155
You ought to be ashamed, I said, to look so antique.
(And her only thirty-one.)
I can't help it, she said, pulling a long face,
It's them pills I took, to bring it off,[30] she said.
(She's had five already, and nearly died of young
                                        George.) 160
The chemist[31] said it would be all right, but I've never
                                        been the same.
You are a proper fool, I said.
Well, if Albert won't leave you alone, there it is, I
                                                    said,
What you get married for if you don't want children?

HURRY UP PLEASE ITS TIME
Well, that Sunday Albert was home, they had a hot
gammon,[32] 165
And they asked me in to dinner, to get the beauty of
it hot—
HURRY UP PLEASE ITS TIME
HURRY UP PLEASE ITS TIME
Goonight Bill. Goonight Lou. Goonight May.
Goonight. 170
Ta ta. Goonight. Goonight.
Good night, ladies, good night, sweet ladies, good
night, good night.[33]

III.
THE FIRE SERMON[34]

The river's tent is broken: the last fingers of leaf
Clutch and sink into the wet bank. The wind
Crosses the brown land, unheard. The nymphs are
departed. 175
Sweet Thames, run softly, till I end my song.[35]
The river bears no empty bottles, sandwich papers,
Silk handkerchiefs, cardboard boxes, cigarette ends

Or other testimony of summer nights. The nymphs
                              are departed.
And their friends, the loitering heirs of city
                              directors;[36] 180
Departed, have left no addresses.
By the waters of Leman I sat down and wept . . .[37]
Sweet Thames, run softly till I end my song,
Sweet Thames, run softly, for I speak not loud or
                              long.
But at my back in a cold blast I hear[38] 185
The rattle of the bones, and chuckle spread from ear
                              to ear.
A rat crept softly through the vegetation
Dragging its slimy belly on the bank
While I was fishing in the dull canal
On a winter evening round behind the gashouse 190
Musing upon the king my brother's wreck
And on the king my father's death before him.[39]
White bodies naked on the low damp ground
And bones cast in a little low dry garret,
Rattled by the rat's foot only, year to year. 195
But at my back from time to time I hear
The sound of horns and motors, which shall bring
Sweeney to Mrs. Porter in the spring.[40]
O the moon shone bright on Mrs. Porter
And on her daughter 200
They wash their feet in soda water
Et O ces voix d'enfants, chantant dans la coupole![41]

Twit twit twit
Jug jug jug jug jug jug
So rudely forc'd.   205
Tereu[42]

  Unreal City
Under the brown fog of a winter noon
Mr. Eugenides, the Smyrna[43] merchant
Unshaven, with a pocket full of currants   210
C.i.f. London:[44] documents at sight,
Asked me in demotic[45] French
To luncheon at the Cannon Street Hotel[46]
Followed by a weekend at the Metropole.

  At the violet hour, when the eyes and back   215
Turn upward from the desk, when the human engine
                                                              waits
Like a taxi throbbing waiting,
I Tiresias, though blind, throbbing between two
                                                              lives,[47]
Old man with wrinkled female breasts, can see
At the violet hour, the evening hour that strives   220
Homeward, and brings the sailor home from sea,[48]
The typist home at teatime, clears her breakfast,
                                                              lights
Her stove, and lays out food in tins.
Out of the window perilously spread
Her drying combinations[49] touched by the sun's last
                                                              rays, 225

On the divan are piled (at night her bed)
Stockings, slippers, camisoles, and stays.[50]
I Tiresias, old man with wrinkled dugs[51]
Perceived the scene, and foretold the rest—
I too awaited the expected guest.   230
He, the young man carbuncular,[52] arrives,
A small house agent's clerk, with one bold stare,
One of the low on whom assurance sits
As a silk hat on a Bradford millionaire.[53]
The time is now propitious, as he guesses,   235
The meal is ended, she is bored and tired,
Endeavours to engage her in caresses
Which still are unreproved, if undesired.
Flushed and decided, he assaults at once;
Exploring hands encounter no defence;   240
His vanity requires no response,
And makes a welcome of indifference.
(And I Tiresias have foresuffered all
Enacted on this same divan or bed;
I who have sat by Thebes below the wall   245
And walked among the lowest of the dead.)[54]
Bestows one final patronising kiss,
And gropes his way, finding the stairs unlit . . .

   She turns and looks a moment in the glass,
Hardly aware of her departed lover;   250
Her brain allows one half-formed thought to pass:
"Well now that's done: and I'm glad it's over."

When lovely woman stoops to folly and
Paces about her room again, alone,
She smoothes her hair with automatic hand,   255
And puts a record on the gramophone.[55]

  "This music crept by me upon the waters"
And along the Strand,[56] up Queen Victoria Street.
O City city, I can sometimes hear
Beside a public bar in Lower Thames Street,   260
The pleasant whining of a mandoline
And a clatter and a chatter from within
Where fishmen lounge at noon: where the walls
Of Magnus Martyr[57] hold
Inexplicable splendour of Ionian white and gold.   265

        The river sweats
Oil and tar
The barges drift
With the turning tide
Red sails   270
Wide
To leeward, swing on the heavy spar.
The barges wash
Drifting logs
Down Greenwich reach[58]   275
Past the Isle of Dogs.[59]
                Weialala leia
                Wallala leialala[60]

Elizabeth and Leicester[61]
Beating oars   280
The stern was formed
A gilded shell
Red and gold
The brisk swell   285
Rippled both shores
Southwest wind
Carried down stream
The peal of bells
White towers
             Weialala leia   290
             Wallala leialala

"Trams[62] and dusty trees.
Highbury bore me. Richmond and Kew
Undid me.[63] By Richmond I raised my knees
Supine on the floor of a narrow canoe."

"My feet are at Moorgate,[64] and my heart   295
Under my feet. After the event
He wept. He promised 'a new start.'
I made no comment. What should I resent?"

"On Margate Sands.[65]   300
I can connect
Nothing with nothing.
The broken fingernails of dirty hands.

My people humble people who expect
Nothing."   305
              la la

  To Carthage then I came[66]

  Burning burning burning burning[67]
O Lord Thou pluckest me out[68]
O Lord Thou pluckest   310

burning

_____

IV.
DEATH BY WATER[69]

Phlebas the Phoenician, a fortnight dead,
Forgot the cry of gulls, and the deep sea swell
And the profit and loss.
                        A current under sea   315
Picked his bones in whispers. As he rose and fell
He passed the stages of his age and youth
Entering the whirlpool.
                        Gentile or Jew
O you who turn the wheel and look to windward,   320
Consider Phlebas, who was once handsome and tall
                                            as you.

V.
WHAT THE THUNDER SAID[70]

After the torchlight red on sweaty faces
After the frosty silence in the gardens
After the agony in stony places
The shouting and the crying   325
Prison and palace and reverberation
Of thunder of spring over distant mountains
He who was living is now dead[71]
We who were living are now dying
With a little patience   330

   Here is no water but only rock
Rock and no water and the sandy road
The road winding above among the mountains
Which are mountains of rock without water
If there were water we should stop and drink   335
Amongst the rock one cannot stop or think
Sweat is dry and feet are in the sand
If there were only water amongst the rock
Dead mountain mouth of carious[72] teeth that cannot
                                     spit
Here one can neither stand nor lie nor sit   340
There is not even silence in the mountains
But dry sterile thunder without rain
There is not even solitude in the mountains

But red sullen faces sneer and snarl
From doors of mudcracked houses   345
                        If there were water

  And no rock
  If there were rock
  And also water
  And water   350
  A spring
  A pool among the rock
  If there were the sound of water only
  Not the cicada
  And dry grass singing   355
  But sound of water over a rock
  Where the hermit-thrush sings in the pine trees
  Drip drop drip drop drop drop drop
  But there is no water

  Who is the third who walks always beside you?[73]   360
When I count, there are only you and I together
But when I look ahead up the white road
There is always another one walking beside you
Gliding wrapt in a brown mantle, hooded
I do not know whether a man or a woman   365
—But who is that on the other side of you?

  What is that sound high in the air
Murmur of maternal lamentation
Who are those hooded hordes swarming

Over endless plains, stumbling in cracked earth   370
Ringed by the flat horizon only
What is the city over the mountains
Cracks and reforms and bursts in the violet air
Falling towers
Jerusalem Athens Alexandria   375
Vienna London
Unreal

A woman drew her long black hair out tight
And fiddled whisper music on those strings
And bats with baby faces in the violet light   380
Whistled, and beat their wings
And crawled head downward down a blackened
                                        wall
And upside down in air were towers
Tolling reminiscent bells, that kept the hours
And voices singing out of empty cisterns and
                                        exhausted wells.   385

In this decayed hole among the mountains
In the faint moonlight, the grass is singing
Over the tumbled graves, about the chapel
There is the empty chapel,[74] only the wind's home.
It has no windows, and the door swings,   390
Dry bones can harm no one.
Only a cock stood on the rooftree
Co co rico co co rico

In a flash of lightning. Then a damp gust
Bringing rain   395

  Ganga[75] was sunken, and the limp leaves
Waited for rain, while the black clouds
Gathered far distant, over Himavant.[76]
The jungle crouched, humped in silence.
Then spoke the thunder   400
DA
Datta:[77] what have we given?
My friend, blood shaking my heart
The awful daring of a moment's surrender
Which an age of prudence can never retract   405
By this, and this only, we have existed
Which is not to be found in our obituaries
Or in memories draped by the beneficent spider
Or under seals broken by the lean solicitor
In our empty rooms   410·
DA
Dayadhvam:[78] I have heard the key
Turn in the door once and turn once only
We think of the key, each in his prison
Thinking of the key, each confirms a prison   415
Only at nightfall, aethereal rumours
Revive for a moment a broken Coriolanus[79]
DA
Damyata:[80] The boat responded
Gaily, to the hand expert with sail and oar   420

The sea was calm, your heart would have responded
Gaily, when invited, beating obedient
To controlling hands

                 I sat upon the shore
Fishing,[81] with the arid plain behind me   425
Shall I at least set my lands in order?[82]
London Bridge is falling down falling down falling
                         down

Poi s'ascose nel foco che gli affina[83]
Quando fiam uti chelidon[84]—O swallow swallow
Le Prince d'Aquitaine à la tour abolie[85]   430
These fragments I have shored against my ruins
Why then Ile fit you. Hieronymo's mad againe.[86]
Datta. Dayadhvam. Damyata.
        Shantih   shantih   shantih[87]

                         (1922)

NOTES ON
"THE WASTE LAND"[88]

Not only the title, but the plan and a good deal of the inci-
dental symbolism of the poem were suggested by Miss
Jessie L. Weston's book on the Grail legend: *From Ritual to*

Romance (Cambridge). Indeed, so deeply am I indebted, Miss Weston's book will elucidate the difficulties of the poem much better than my notes can do; and I recommend it (apart from the great interest of the book itself) to any who think such elucidation of the poem worth the trouble. To another work of anthropology I am indebted in general, one which has influenced our generation profoundly; I mean *The Golden Bough*,[89] I have used especially the two volumes *Adonis, Attis, Osiris*.[90] Anyone who is acquainted with these works will immediately recognize in the poem certain references to vegetation ceremonies.

I. THE BURIAL OF THE DEAD

Line 20. Cf. Ezekiel II, i.

23. Cf. Ecclesiastes XII, v.

31. V. Tristan und Isolde, I, verses 5–8.

42. Id. III, verse 24.

46. I am not familiar with the exact constitution of the Tarot pack of cards, from which I have obviously departed to suit my own convenience. The Hanged Man, a member of the traditional pack, fits my purpose in two ways: because he is associated in my mind with the Hanged God of Frazer, and because I associate him with the hooded figure in the passage of the disciples to Emmaus in Part V. The Phoenician Sailor and the Merchant appear later; also the "crowds of people," and Death by Water is executed in Part IV. The Man with Three Staves (an authentic member of the Tarot

pack) I associate, quite arbitrarily, with the Fisher King himself.

60. Cf. Baudelaire:
    "Fourmillante cité, cité pleine de rêves,
    "Où le spectre en plein jour raccroche le passant."[91]

63. Cf. Inferno III, 55–57:
                    "si lunga tratta
    di gente, ch'io non avrei mai creduto
        che morte tanta n'avesse disfatta."[92]

64. Cf. Inferno IV, 25–27:
    "Quivi, secondo che per ascoltare,
    "non avea pianto, ma' che di sospiri,
    "che l'aura eterna facevan tremare."[93]

68. A phenomenon which I have often noticed.

74. Cf. the Dirge in Webster's White Devil.

76. V. Baudelaire, Preface to Fleurs du Mal.

II. A GAME OF CHESS

77. Cf. Antony and Cleopatra, II, ii, l. 190.

92. Laquearia. V. Aeneid, I, 726:
    dependent lychni laquearibus aureis incensi, et noctem flammis funalia vincunt.[94]

98. Sylvan scene. V. Milton, Paradise Lost, IV, 140.

99. V. Ovid, Metamorphoses, VI, Philomela.

100. Cf. Part III, l. 204.

115. Cf. Part III, l. 195.

118. Cf. Webster: "Is the wind in that door still?"[95]

126. Cf. Part I, l. 37, 48.

138. Cf. the game of chess in Middleton's *Women beware Women*.[96]

III. THE FIRE SERMON

176. V. Spenser, *Prothalamion*.

192. Cf. *The Tempest*, I, ii.

196. Cf. Marvell, *To His Coy Mistress*.

197. Cf. Day, *Parliament of Bees*:

"When of the sudden, listening, you shall hear,
"A noise of horns and hunting, which shall bring
"Actaeon to Diana in the spring,
"Where all shall see her naked skin . . ."

199. I do not know the origin of the ballad from which these lines are taken: it was reported to me from Sydney, Australia.

202. V. Verlaine, *Parsifal*.

210. The currants were quoted at a price "carriage and insurance free to London"; and the Bill of Lading etc. were to be handed to the buyer upon payment of the sight draft.

218. Tiresias, although a mere spectator and not indeed a "character," is yet the most important personage in the poem, uniting all the rest. Just as the one-eyed merchant, seller of currants, melts into the Phoenician Sailor, and the latter is not wholly distinct from Ferdinand Prince of Na-

ples,[97] so all the women are one woman, and the two sexes meet in Tiresias. What Tiresias *sees*, in fact, is the substance of the poem. The whole passage from Ovid is of great anthropological interest:

'. . . Cum Iunone iocos et maior vestra profecto est Quam, quae contingit maribus,' dixisse, 'voluptas.' Illa negat; placuit quae sit sententia docti Quaerere Tiresiae: venus huic erat utraque nota. Nam duo magnorum viridi coeuntia silva Corpora serpentum baculi violaverat ictu Deque viro factus, mirabile, femina septem Egerat autumnos; octavo rursus eosdem Vidit et 'est vestrae si tanta potentia plagae,' Dixit 'ut auctoris sortem in contraria mutet, Nunc quoque vos feriam!' percussis anguibus isdem Forma prior rediit genetivaque venit imago. Arbiter hic igitur sumptus de lite iocosa Dicta Iovis firmat; gravius Saturnia iusto Nec pro materia fertur doluisse suique Iudicis aeterna damnavit lumina nocte, At pater omnipotens (neque enim licet inrita cuiquam Facta dei fecisse deo) pro lumine adempto Scire futura dedit poenamque levavit honore.[98]

221. This may not appear as exact as Sappho's lines, but I had in mind the "longshore" or "dory" fisherman, who returns at nightfall.

253. V. Goldsmith, the song in *The Vicar of Wakefield.*

257. V. *The Tempest,* as above.

264. The interior of St. Magnus Martyr is to my mind one of the finest among Wren's interiors. See *The Proposed Demolition of Nineteen City Churches:* (P. S. King & Son, Ltd.).

266. The Song of the (three) Thames-daughters begins here. From line 292 to 306 inclusive they speak in turn. V. *Götterdämmerung*, III, i: the Rhine-daughters.

279. V. Froude, *Elizabeth*, Vol. I, ch. iv, letter of De Quadra to Philip of Spain:

"In the afternoon we were in a barge, watching the games on the river. (The queen) was alone with Lord Robert and myself on the poop, when they began to talk nonsense, and went so far that Lord Robert at last said, as I was on the spot there was no reason why they should not be married if the queen pleased."

293. Cf. *Purgatorio*, V, 133:

"Ricorditi di me, che son la Pia;

"Siena mi fe', disfecemi Maremma.'"

307. V. St. Augustine's *Confessions:* "to Carthage then I came, where a cauldron of unholy loves sang all about mine ears."

308. The complete text of the Buddha's Fire Sermon (which corresponds in importance to the Sermon on the Mount) from which these words are taken, will be found translated in the late Henry Clarke Warren's *Buddhism in Translation* (Harvard Oriental Series). Mr. Warren was one of the great pioneers of Buddhist studies in the Occident.

309. From St. Augustine's *Confessions* again. The collocation of these two representatives of eastern and western asceticism, as the culmination of this part of the poem, is not an accident.

V. WHAT THE THUNDER SAID

In the first part of Part V three themes are employed: the journey to Emmaus, the approach to the Chapel Perilous (see Miss Weston's book) and the present decay of eastern Europe.

357. This is *Turdus aonalaschkae pallasii*, the hermit-thrush which I have heard in Quebec Province. Chapman says (*Handbook of Birds of Eastern North America*) "it is most at home in secluded woodland and thickety retreats. . . . Its notes are not remarkable for variety or volume, but in purity and sweetness of tone and exquisite modulation they are unequalled." Its "water-dripping song" is justly celebrated.

360. The following lines were stimulated by the account of one of the Antarctic expeditions (I forget which, but I think one of Shackleton's): it was related that the party of explorers, at the extremity of their strength, had the constant delusion that there was *one more member* than could actually be counted.

367–77. Cf. Hermann Hesse, *Blick ins Chaos*: "Schon ist halb Europa, schon ist zumindest der halbe Osten Europas auf dem Wege zum Chaos, fährt betrunken im heiligem Wahn am Abgrund entlang und singt dazu, singt betrunken und hymnisch wie Dmitri Karamasoff sang. Ueber diese Lieder lacht der Bürger beleidigt, der Heilige und Seher hört sie mit Tränen."[100]

402. "Datta, dayadhvam, damyata" (Give, sympathise, control). The fable of the meaning of the Thunder is found

in the *Brihadaranyaka—Upanishad*, 5, 1. A translation is found in Deussen's *Sechzig Upanishads des Veda*, p. 489.

    408. Cf. Webster, *The White Devil*, V, vi:

>   "... they'll remarry
> Ere the worm pierce your winding-sheet, ere the
>   spider
> Make a thin curtain for your epitaphs."

    412. Cf. *Inferno*, XXXIII, 46:

> "ed io sentii chiavar l'uscio di sotto
> all'orribile torre."[101]

    Also F. H. Bradley, *Appearance and Reality*, p. 346.

'My external sensations are no less private to myself than are my thoughts or my feelings. In either case my experience falls within my own circle, a circle closed on the outside, and, with all its elements alike, every sphere is opaque to the others which surround it. . . . In brief, regarded as an existence which appears in a soul, the whole world for each is peculiar and private to that soul.'

    425. V. Weston: *From Ritual to Romance;* chapter on the Fisher King.

    428. V. *Purgatorio*, XXVI, 148.

> " 'Ara vos prec per aquella valor
> 'que vos guida al som de l'escalina,
> 'sovegna vos a temps de ma dolor.'
> Poi s'ascose nel foco che gli affina."

    429. V. *Pervigilium Veneris*. Cf. Philomela in Parts II and III.

    430. V. Gerard de Nerval, Sonnet *El Desdichado*.

    432. V. Kyd's *Spanish Tragedy*.

434. Shantih. Repeated as here, a formal ending to an Upanishad. "The Peace which passeth understanding" is our equivalent to this word.

THE HOLLOW MEN[1]

Mistah Kurtz—he dead.[2]

A penny for the Old Guy[3]

I

We are the hollow men
We are the stuffed men
Leaning together
Headpiece filled with straw. Alas!
Our dried voices, when   5
We whisper together
Are quiet and meaningless
As wind in dry grass
Or rats' feet over broken glass
In our dry cellar   10

   Shape without form, shade without colour,
Paralysed force, gesture without motion;

Those who have crossed
With direct eyes, to death's other Kingdom
Remember us—if at all—not as lost   15
Violent souls, but only
As the hollow men
The stuffed men.

II

Eyes I dare not meet in dreams
In death's dream kingdom   20
These do not appear:
There, the eyes are
Sunlight on a broken column
There, is a tree swinging
And voices are   25
In the wind's singing
More distant and more solemn
Than a fading star.

Let me be no nearer
In death's dream kingdom   30
Let me also wear
Such deliberate disguises
Rat's coat, crowskin, crossed staves

In a field
Behaving as the wind behaves   35
No nearer—

   Not that final meeting
In the twilight kingdom

III

This is the dead land
This is cactus land   40
Here the stone images
Are raised, here they receive
The supplication of a dead man's hand
Under the twinkle of a fading star.

   Is it like this   45
In death's other kingdom
Waking alone
At the hour when we are
Trembling with tenderness
Lips that would kiss   50
Form prayers to broken stone.

IV

The eyes are not here
There are no eyes here
In this valley of dying stars
In this hollow valley   55
This broken jaw of our lost kingdoms

  In this last of meeting places
We grope together
And avoid speech
Gathered on this beach of the tumid river   60

  Sightless, unless
The eyes reappear
As the perpetual star
Multifoliate rose[4]
Of death's twilight kingdom   65
The hope only
Of empty men.

V

Here we go round the prickly pear[5]
Prickly pear prickly pear
Here we go round the prickly pear   70
At five o'clock in the morning.

  Between the idea
And the reality
Between the motion
And the act   75
Falls the Shadow

                  For Thine is the Kingdom

  Between the conception
And the creation
Between the emotion   80
And the response
Falls the Shadow

                  Life is very long

  Between the desire
And the spasm   85
Between the potency
And the existence
Between the essence
And the descent
Falls the Shadow   90

                  For Thine is the Kingdom

For Thine⁶ is
Life is
For Thine is the

This is the way the world ends 95
This is the way the world ends
This is the way the world ends
Not with a bang but a whimper.

(1925)

ASH-WEDNESDAY[1]

I

Because I do not hope to turn again
Because I do not hope
Because I do not hope to turn
Desiring this man's gift and that man's scope
I no longer strive to strive towards such things   5
(Why should the agèd eagle stretch its wings?)
Why should I mourn
The vanished power of the usual reign?

  Because I do not hope to know again
The infirm glory of the positive hour   10
Because I do not think
Because I know I shall not know
The one veritable transitory power
Because I cannot drink
There, where trees flower, and springs flow, for there
                             is nothing again   15

Because I know that time is always time
And place is always and only place
And what is actual is actual only for one time
And only for one place
I rejoice that things are as they are and   20
I renounce the blessèd face
And renounce the voice
Because I cannot hope to turn again
Consequently I rejoice, having to construct
                                            something
Upon which to rejoice   25

    And pray to God to have mercy upon us
And I pray that I may forget
These matters that with myself I too much discuss
Too much explain
Because I do not hope to turn again   30
Let these words answer
For what is done, not to be done again
May the judgement not be too heavy upon us

    Because these wings are no longer wings to fly
But merely vans to beat the air   35
The air which is now thoroughly small and dry
Smaller and dryer than the will
Teach us to care and not to care
Teach us to sit still.

Pray for us[2] sinners now and at the hour of our
                                          death   40
Pray for us now and at the hour of our death.

II

Lady,[3] three white leopards sat under a juniper-tree
In the cool of the day, having fed to satiety
On my legs my heart my liver and that which had
                              been contained
In the hollow round of my skull. And God said   45
Shall these bones live? shall these
Bones live? And that which had been contained
In the bones (which were already dry) said chirping:
Because of the goodness of this Lady
And because of her loveliness, and because   50
She honours the Virgin in meditation,
We shine with brightness. And I who am here
                              dissembled
Proffer my deeds to oblivion, and my love
To the posterity of the desert and the fruit of the
                              gourd.
It is this which recovers   55
My guts the strings of my eyes and the indigestible
                              portions

Which the leopards reject. The Lady is withdrawn
In a white gown, to contemplation, in a white gown.
Let the whiteness of bones atone to forgetfulness.
There is no life in them. As I am forgotten   60
And would be forgotten, so I would forget
Thus devoted, concentrated in purpose. And God
                                              said
Prophesy to the wind, to the wind only for only
The wind will listen. And the bones sang chirping
With the burden of the grasshopper, saying   65

Lady of silences
Calm and distressed
Torn and most whole
Rose of memory
Rose of forgetfulness   70
Exhausted and life-giving
Worried reposeful
The single Rose
Is now the Garden
Where all loves end   75
Terminate torment
Of love unsatisfied
The greater torment
Of love satisfied
End of the endless   80
Journey to no end
Conclusion of all that

Is inconclusible
Speech without word and
Word of no speech   85
Grace to the Mother
For the Garden
Where all love ends.

  Under a juniper-tree the bones sang, scattered and
                                                 shining
We are glad to be scattered, we did little good to each
                                                  other,   90
Under a tree in the cool of the day, with the blessing
                                                 of sand,
Forgetting themselves and each other, united
In the quiet of the desert. This is the land which ye
Shall divide by lot. And neither division nor unity
Matters. This is the land. We have our inheritance.   95

III

At the first turning of the second stair
I turned and saw below
The same shape twisted on the banister
Under the vapour in the fetid air
Struggling with the devil of the stairs who wears   100
The deceitful face of hope and of despair.

   At the second turning of the second stair
I left them twisting, turning below;
There were no more faces and the stair was dark,
Damp, jaggèd, like an old man's mouth drivelling,
                        beyond repair,   105
Or the toothed gullet of an agèd shark.

   At the first turning of the third stair
Was a slotted window bellied like the fig's fruit
And beyond the hawthorn blossom and a pasture
                              scene
The broadbacked figure drest in blue and green   110
Enchanted the maytime with an antique flute.
Blown hair is sweet, brown hair over the mouth
                              blown,
Lilac and brown hair;
Distraction, music of the flute, stops and steps of the
                    mind over the third stair,
Fading, fading; strength beyond hope and despair   115
Climbing the third stair.

   Lord, I am not worthy
Lord, I am not worthy

      but speak the word only.

IV

Who walked between the violet and the violet   120
Who walked between
The various ranks of varied green
Going in white and blue, in Mary's colour,
Talking of trivial things
In ignorance and in knowledge of eternal dolour   125
Who moved among the others as they walked,
Who then made strong the fountains and made fresh
                     the springs

  Made cool the dry rock and made firm the sand
In blue of larkspur, blue of Mary's colour,
Sovegna vos   130

  Here are the years that walk between, bearing
Away the fiddles and the flutes, restoring
One who moves in the time between sleep and
                    waking, wearing

  White light folded, sheathed about her, folded.
The new years walk, restoring   135
Through a bright cloud of tears, the years, restoring
With a new verse the ancient rhyme. Redeem
The time. Redeem
The unread vision in the higher dream
While jewelled unicorns draw by the gilded hearse.   140

The silent sister veiled in white and blue
Between the yews, behind the garden god,
Whose flute is breathless, bent her head and signed
                                but spoke no word

But the fountain sprang up and the bird sang
                                down
Redeem the time, redeem the dream   145
The token of the word unheard, unspoken

Till the wind shake a thousand whispers from the
                                yew

And after this our exile

<hr>

V

If the lost word is lost, if the spent word is spent
If the unheard, unspoken   150
Word is unspoken, unheard;
Still is the unspoken word, the Word unheard,
The Word without a word, the Word within
The world and for the world;
And the light shone in darkness and   155
Against the Word the unstilled world still whirled
About the centre of the silent Word.

O my people, what have I done unto thee.

Where shall the word be found, where will the
word

Resound? Not here, there is not enough silence   160
Not on the sea or on the islands, not
On the mainland, in the desert or the rain land,
For those who walk in darkness
Both in the day time and in the night time
The right time and the right place are not here   165
No place of grace for those who avoid the face
No time to rejoice for those who walk among noise
and deny the voice

Will the veiled sister pray for
Those who walk in darkness, who chose thee and
oppose thee,
Those who are torn on the horn between season and
season, time and time, between   170
Hour and hour, word and word, power and power,
those who walk
In darkness? Will the veiled sister pray
For children at the gate
Who will not go away and cannot pray:
Pray for those who chose and oppose   175

O my people, what have I done unto thee.

Will the veiled sister between the slender
Yew trees pray for those who offend her

And are terrified and cannot surrender
And affirm before the world and deny between the
rocks 180
In the last desert between the last blue rocks
The desert in the garden the garden in the desert
Of drouth, spitting from the mouth the withered
apple-seed.

    O my people.

VI

Although I do not hope to turn again   185
Although I do not hope
Although I do not hope to turn

   Wavering between the profit and the loss
In this brief transit where the dreams cross
The dreamcrossed twilight between birth and dying   190
(Bless me father) though I do not wish to wish these
things
From the wide window towards the granite shore
The white sails still fly seaward, seaward flying
Unbroken wings

   And the lost heart stiffens and rejoices   195
In the lost lilac and the lost sea voices

And the weak spirit quickens to rebel
For the bent golden-rod and the lost sea smell
Quickens to recover
The cry of quail and the whirling plover   200
And the blind eye creates
The empty forms between the ivory gates
And smell renews the salt savour of the sandy earth

   This is the time of tension between dying and birth
The place of solitude where three dreams cross   205
Between blue rocks
But when the voices shaken from the yew-tree drift
                     away
Let the other yew be shaken and reply.

   Blessèd sister, holy mother, spirit of the fountain,
                 spirit of the garden,
Suffer us not to mock ourselves with falsehood   210
Teach us to care and not to care
Teach us to sit still
Even among these rocks,
Our peace in His will
And even among these rocks   215
Sister, mother
And spirit of the river, spirit of the sea,
Suffer me not to be separated

   And let my cry come unto Thee.

                          (1930)

JOURNEY OF THE MAGI[1]

'A cold coming we had of it,
Just the worst time of the year
For a journey, and such a long journey:
The ways deep and the weather sharp,
The very dead of winter.'   5
And the camels galled, sore-footed, refractory,
Lying down in the melting snow.
There were times we regretted
The summer palaces on slopes, the terraces,
And the silken girls bringing sherbet.   10
Then the camel men cursing and grumbling
And running away, and wanting their liquor and
                                            women,
And the night-fires going out, and the lack of
                                            shelters,
And the cities hostile and the towns unfriendly
And the villages dirty and charging high prices: 15
A hard time we had of it.
At the end we preferred to travel all night,
Sleeping in snatches,

With the voices singing in our ears, saying
That this was all folly.   20

· Then at dawn we came down to a temperate valley,
Wet, below the snow line, smelling of vegetation;
With a running stream and a water-mill beating the
                                                        darkness,
And three trees on the low sky,
And an old white horse galloped away in the
                                                        meadow. 25
Then we came to a tavern with vine-leaves over the
                                                        lintel,
Six hands at an open door dicing for pieces of silver,
And feet kicking the empty wine-skins.
But there was no information, and so we continued
And arrived at evening, not a moment too soon   30
Finding the place; it was (you may say) satisfactory.

    All this was a long time ago, I remember,
And I would do it again, but set down
This set down
This: were we led all that way for   35
Birth or Death? There was a Birth, certainly,
We had evidence and no doubt. I had seen birth and
                                                        death,
But had thought they were different; this Birth was
Hard and bitter agony for us, like Death, our death.
We returned to our places, these Kingdoms,   40

But no longer at ease here, in the old dispensation,
With an alien people clutching their gods.
I should be glad of another death.

FROM *FIVE-FINGER EXERCISES*

V.
LINES FOR CUSCUSCARAWAY AND
MIRZA MURAD ALI BEG

How unpleasant to meet Mr. Eliot!
With his features of clerical cut,
And his brow so grim
And his mouth so prim
And his conversation, so nicely   5
Restricted to What Precisely
And If and Perhaps and But.
How unpleasant to meet Mr. Eliot!
With a bobtail cur
In a coat of fur   10
And a porpentine cat
And a wopsical hat:
How unpleasant to meet Mr. Eliot!
            (Whether his mouth be open or shut).

ANNOTATIONS

―――――

SPLEEN

1. Published in *Poems Written in Early Youth*. Composed around 1910.

THE DEATH OF SAINT NARCISSUS

1. The title represents a conflation of the mythological Narcissus—who fell in love with his own image in a pool and is consequently the symbol of autoeroticism—and Saint Sebastian, a Christian who was martyred by being shot through with arrows. The death of Saint Sebastian was a favorite subject in the Renaissance for painters wishing to depict the male nude.

2. The doctrine of the transmigration of the soul here shows the soul rising in the evolutionary scale as it passes from one body to another.

THE LOVE SONG OF J. ALFRED PRUFROCK

1. From Dante's *Inferno*, XXVII, 61–66. Guido da Montefeltro speaks, after Dante questions him: "If I thought that my reply were to be to someone who would ever return to the world, this flame would be still, without further motion. But since no one has ever returned alive from this depth, if what I hear is true, I answer you without fear of shame." In the poem, Prufrock speaks, similarly, an inner truth to an unnamed "you."

2. The Greek poet Hesiod (eighth century B.C.) wrote *Works and Days*, a georgic poem.

3. The head of John the Baptist was delivered on a platter to Salome (Matthew 14:1–11).

4. Lazarus was raised from the dead by Jesus (John 11:1–44).

5. I.e., Prufrock will be, not like Hamlet the hero, but rather like Polonius, a fussy court advisor.

6. Royal procession.

7. Sententiousness.

PRELUDES

1. From *Prufrock and Other Observations*.

THE *BOSTON EVENING TRANSCRIPT*

1. From *Prufrock and Other Observations.*

HYSTERIA

1. From *Prufrock and Other Observations.*

LA FIGLIA CHE PIANGE

1. Italian: "The Weeping Girl."
2. From Virgil's *Aeneid*, I, 327: "By what name shall I call thee, O maiden?" This is Aeneas' salutation to the huntress who is in fact his mother, Venus.

GERONTION

1. From *Poems 1920*. The title is from the Greek for "little old man," and is pronounced with a hard *g*.
2. "Thou hast . . ." Shakespeare, *Measure for Measure* III.i.
3. Site of the Spartan loss to an invading Persian army, 480 B.C.
4. French: "excrement."
5. Cf. Lancelot Andrewes' (1555–1626) commentary on the Gospels in *Works I*, 204.
6. The constellation in the Northern sky.

7. The gull attempts difficult passage to the North (the Belle Isle Straits off the eastern shore of Canada) and the South (Cape Horn) while Gerontion sails easily with the trade winds.

THE HIPPOPOTAMUS

1. From *Poems 1920*. "Similiter . . ." (epigraph) from Saint Ignatius to the Trallians. "In like manner let all reverence the Deacons as Jesus Christ and the Bishop as the Father and the presbyters as the council o God, and the assembly of apostles. Without these there is no Church. About these things I am sure you agree."

WHISPERS OF IMMORTALITY

1. John Webster, English dramatist (1580?–1634) and the author of the play *The Duchess of Malfi* (c. 1614).

SWEENEY AMONG THE NIGHTINGALES

1. "Alas, I am struck a mortal blow within" (epigraph), Agamemnon's cry as he is murdered by his wife and her lover (Aeschylus, *Agamemnon*, I. 1343).

2. Sweeney, with his apelike neck and gorillalike arms, is Eliot's figure for brutish man.

3. Spotted.
4. In Argentina.
5. In Hades, the gate through which true dreams pass.
6. The constellation Orion and the Dog Star, Sirius.

THE WASTE LAND

1. "For I myself saw with my own eyes the Cumaean Sibyl hanging in a bottle, and when the boys said to her, 'Sibyl, what do you want?,' she would reply, 'I want to die'" (Petronius, *Satyricon*, XLVIII). The Sibyl, in requesting longevity from Apollo, had forgotten to ask for perpetual youth and had therefore shriveled with age.

2. "The better craftsman" (Dante, *Purgatorio*, XXVI, 117). Eliot's tribute to Pound, whose editorial help can be seen in the facsimile *Waste Land* (1971), which transcribes the original manuscript of the poem.

3. Title of the funeral service in the Anglican *Book of Common Prayer*.

4. Lake near Munich.

5. Park in Munich.

6. German: "I'm not Russian at all, I come from Lithuania, pure German."

7. God's address to the prophet Ezekiel (E.,I,20).

8. "The grasshopper shall be a burden" in old age, when "desire shall fail," says the Preacher in Ecclesiastes (E.,I,23).

9. Cf. Isaiah 32:1–2, where the coming of the Messiah will be "as the shadow of a great rock in a weary land."

10. "Dust thou art, and unto dust thou shalt return," as in the funeral service.

11. From Richard Wagner's opera *Tristan und Isolde* (E.,I,34), the young steersman's lyric song: "The wind blows fresh / To the homeland / My Irish girl, / Where are you waiting?"

12. "Empty and barren the sea" (E.,I,42), Tristan's lament as he lies dying, thinking that he will die before Isolde arrives.

13. Tarot cards, used to tell fortunes (E.,I,46).

14. From Shakespeare's *The Tempest* (Act I, Sc. ii, l. 398); said of a drowned father.

15. Quoted from Dante's *Inferno* (E.,I,63).

16. London church.

17. Naval battle (260 B.C.) in which the Romans defeated the Carthaginians.

18. An echo from the play *The White Devil* (1612) by John Webster. The original reads: "But keep the wolf far thence, that's foe to men, / For with his nails he'll dig them up again" (Act V, Sc. iv, ll. 97–98).

19. From Baudelaire's poem "Au Lecteur" ("To the Reader"): "Hypocrite reader!—my double,—my brother!" (E.,I,76).

20. Title of a play by Thomas Middleton (1627) about a marriage of convenience.

21. Echo of a passage in Shakespeare's *Antony and Cleopatra* (Act II, Sc. ii, ll. 196–197), referring to Cleopatra's barge: "The barge she sat in, like a burnish'd throne, / Burn'd on the water."

22. Statue of Cupid, god of love in Roman mythology.

23. Paneled ceiling as described in a passage in Virgil's *Aeneid* telling of Dido's welcome of Aeneas to Carthage. When Aeneas left her, Dido committed suicide (E.,II,92).

24. Allusion to the Garden of Eden in John Milton's *Paradise Lost* (IV, 140).

25. Ovid, in the *Metamorphoses*, retells the story of the rape of Philomel by her brother-in-law Tereus; he cut out her tongue, but the gods, in compensation, turned her into a nightingale.

26. Conventional Elizabethan rendering of the nightingale's song.

27. Lines adapted from a popular song, "That Shakesperian Rag."

28. Demobilized from the army (slang).

29. English pubkeeper's announcement of closing time.

30. I.e., to cause an abortion.

31. In England: "pharmacist."

32. Bacon.

33. From Ophelia's mad speech, after Hamlet has repudiated her (Shakespeare's *Hamlet*, Act IV, Sc. ii, ll. 72–74).

34. Title of a sermon by the Buddha, denouncing the fires of passion, hatred, and infatuation with which the senses burn (E.,III,308).

35. From Edmund Spenser's "Prothalamion," a nuptial eulogy describing a wedding party on the river Thames, including nymphs and swans.

36. The "city" is London's financial district.

37. Echo of Psalm 137, lamenting the Jews' exile from Jerusalem: "By the rivers of Babylon, there we sat down, yea, we wept, when we remembered Zion." Eliot substitutes

"Leman," the French name for Lake Geneva. (Eliot was hospitalized in Lausanne, Switzerland, while writing *The Waste Land*.)

38. Adapted from "To His Coy Mistress" by Andrew Marvell (1621–1678): "But at my back I always hear / Time's wingèd chariot hurrying near."

39. Adapted from Shakespeare's *Tempest* (Act I, Sc. ii, ll. 389–391), as Ferdinand laments his father's presumed death: "Sitting on a bank, / Weeping against the king my father's wreck, / This music crept by me upon the waters."

40. Sweeney, as in Eliot's other poems, represents vulgar humanity. Mrs. Porter and her daughter appear in a bawdy song from World War I. The allusion (E.,III,197) is to a poem by John Day (1574–1640?) that mentions Actaeon's violation of the goddess Diana's privacy as he spied on her as she was bathing, an offense that was punished by death.

41. French: "And O those treble voices, singing in the dome!" This is the closing line of the sonnet "Parsifal" by Paul Verlaine (1844–1896). In Wagner's opera *Parsifal*, the voices of boy sopranos are heard up high, from the wings, in the final affirmation of Parsifal's salvation once he has defeated the seductress Kundry, thereby preserving his sexual purity.

42. A reprise of the nightingale's song and the story of Philomel and Tereus.

43. Turkish port.

44. "Carriage and insurance free" to London.

45. Vulgar.

46. Presumably, a homosexual assignation in a luxury hotel in Brighton.

47. Tiresias, a blind prophet, had been transformed into a woman for seven years; when asked by the gods who had greater pleasure in sex, men or women, he answered that it was women (E.,III,218).

48. The allusion is to Sappho's poem (CXLIX) on the evening star, which brings all things home that the morning had dispersed.

49. Underwear.

50. Corsets.

51. Breasts.

52. I.e., suffering from acne.

53. A *nouveau riche* industrialist from Bradford, Yorkshire.

54. Tiresias lived in Thebes, and in the afterlife in Hades.

55. Echo of *The Vicar of Wakefield* by Oliver Goldsmith (1728–1774), in which Olivia recalls her seduction: "When lovely woman stoops to folly, / And finds too late that men betray, / What charm can soothe her melancholy? / What art can wash her guilt away?"

56. London street.

57. London church built by the famous architect Sir Christopher Wren (1632–1723) (E.,III,264).

58. Along the Thames River at Greenwich.

59. Peninsula in the Thames opposite Greenwich where Queen Elizabeth I was born.

60. From the song of the Rhinemaidens in Wagner's *Ring* cycle. These are the river nymphs who open the tetralogy and who repossess their Rhinegold at the end.

61. Queen Elizabeth I and Robert Dudley, earl of Leicester. The account of their boat ride on the Thames (E.,III,279)

is drawn from an incident, retold by the Spanish ambassador, in which Elizabeth and Leicester joked about their marrying. Of course no marriage took place.

62. Streetcars.

63. Highbury, Richmond, and Kew are areas near London. The passage rephrases Dante's "Siena bore me; Maremma undid me" (E.,III,64).

64. Slum in East London.

65. Resort on the Thames estuary.

66. From the *Confessions* of St. Augustine; in Carthage, Augustine continued his life of sexual sin (E.,III,309).

67. From the Buddha's Fire Sermon.

68. St. Augustine (*Confessions*) thanks God for having plucked him out of the life of sin.

69. Eliot had dedicated his first volume of verse to the memory of his French friend Jean Verdenal, who had drowned. (See Madame Sosostris's warning [I, 55].)

70. The thunder is the voice of God in the Indian *Upanishads* (E.,V,402).

71. The opening of this section recalls Jesus' agony in the Garden of Gethsemane, his betrayal by Judas, his judging by Pontius Pilate in the palace, and his death.

72. Decayed.

73. Eliot suggests here the hallucinations of Antarctic explorers; he also recalls (E.,V, introductory note) Christ's accompanying, unrecognized, two disciples to Emmaus after his resurrection.

74. In Arthurian legend, the Chapel Perilous, where the Grail knights prayed before they set out to find the Holy Grail.

75. The Ganges, India's sacred river.

76. The Himalayas.

77. Sanskrit for "give," the first word of the thunder in the Upanishads.

78. Sanskrit: "sympathize."

79. Shakespeare's tragic hero who betrayed his own country and then betrayed the opposite camp.

80. Sanskrit: "Control yourselves."

81. Eliot's note refers to the Fisher King of the Grail legend (E.,V,425).

82. Allusion to God's command in Isaiah 38:1: "Set thine house in order; for thou shalt die, and not live."

83. In the *Purgatorio* (*Purgatory*) of Dante's *Divine Comedy*, the Provençal poet Arnaut Daniel implores Dante's regard: "Then he hid himself in the fire that refines them."

84. "When will I be like the swallow" (and have a mate and be able to sing again)? From the late Latin poem *Pervigilium Veneris* (*The Vigil of Venus*), a love complaint (E.,V,429).

85. French: "The prince of Aquitaine of the ruined tower." From the sonnet "El Desdichado" ("The Disinherited Son") by Gérard de Nerval (1808–1855). The passage reads: "I am the man of shadows, the widower, unconsoled, / The prince of Aquitaine of the ruined tower, / My only star is dead, and my starry lute / Bears the black sun of melancholia."

86. Lines from Elizabethan playwright Thomas Kyd's revenge play *The Spanish Tragedy*. "I'll suit your wish," says the bereaved father Hieronymo, agreeing to write a play by means of which, even though mad, he revenges himself for the murder of his son and then kills himself.

87. Sanskrit: the formal ending of an Upanishad; equivalent, says Eliot, to "the peace which passeth understanding" (E.,V,434).

88. In its original appearance in journals in both England and America, *The Waste Land* had no notes. When it appeared as a separate publication, Eliot was asked to fill out the pages and added the notes.

89. Sir James Frazer's compendium of myths and religions (1890).

90. Vegetation gods who die and are reborn.

91. From "Les Sept Vieillards" ("The Seven Old Men") of Charles Baudelaire (1821–1867): "Swarming city, city of dreams, / Where in broad daylight a ghost accosts the passerby."

92. Dante: "such a long train / of people, that I would never have believed / that death had undone so many."

93. Dante: "Here, as far as hearing could ascertain, / was no complaint, except for sighs, / that made the eternal air tremble."

94. "Lighted lamps hang from the gold-paneled ceiling, and flaming torches vanquish the night."

95. In John Webster's play *The Devil's Law-Case* (1623) this is said of a dying man, meaning "Is there still breath coming from his mouth?"

96. In this play by Thomas Middleton (1657), a guardian plays a game of chess while her ward is seduced.

97. In Shakespeare's *The Tempest*.

98. The passage Eliot quotes is from Ovid's *Metamorphoses* II, 421–43: "Jove said jestingly to Juno: 'You wives have

greater pleasure in love than husbands.' She denied it. It pleased them to ask the opinion of the learned Tiresias, who knew both sorts of love. For once, with a blow of his staff, he had separated two copulating snakes in the forest, and was miraculously changed instantly from a man into a woman, remaining so for seven years. In the eighth year he saw the same snakes again and said, 'If striking you is so powerful that it changes the sex of the one dealing the blow, then I will now strike you again.' As soon as he struck them, his former shape and masculine form were restored. As arbiter of the jesting quarrel, he supported Jove's opinion. Juno, disturbed by the decision, decreed that he should be condemned to eternal blindness. But the omnipotent god (since no god can undo what has been done by another god) gave him the power to know the future, with this honor redeeming his loss of sight."

99. La Pia, born in Siena, was murdered by her husband in his castle at Maremma: "Remember me, who am La Pia; / Siena made me, Maremma undid me."

100. "Already half of Europe, already at least half of Eastern Europe, is on the way to chaos, traveling drunken in a sort of holy ecstasy, headlong toward the abyss, singing the while, singing drunken hymns, as Dmitri Karamazov sang. The offended bourgeois laughs at these songs; the saint and the seer hear them with tears."

101. Ugolino was imprisoned with his children, and they starved to death: "And I heard the key turn below in the door / of the horrible tower."

THE HOLLOW MEN

1. Cf. Shakespeare, *Julius Caesar* IV.ii, "But hollow men, like horses hot at hand / Make gallant show and promise of their mettle."

2. "Mistah Kurtz . . ." (first epigraph), cf. Joseph Conrad, *Heart of Darkness*. Kurtz, Conrad's hero, grows corrupt and insane deep in the African jungle.

3. "A penny . . ." (second epigraph), English children's saying. Guy Fawkes' conspiracy to blow up the House of Commons (1605) was thwarted and Fawkes executed. The day of execution, November 5, is celebrated with children making effigies of the "guy" and begging pennies.

4. Dante's vision of Paradise in his *Paradiso*. Souls saved in Heaven arrange themselves around God, like petals falling back from a rose.

5. Eliot's version of the children's game "Here we go round the mulberry bush."

6. "For thine . . ." from the Lord's Prayer.

ASH-WEDNESDAY

1. The title refers to the Christian holy day. The poem draws heavily on Eliot's interest in Dante, and should be read beside his essay "Dante."

2. "Pray for us . . ." from the Ave Maria, the prayer of praise to Mary, mother of Christ.

3. Cf. I Kings 19. Elijah sat under a juniper tree and wished for death.

4. "Lord, I am not worthy . . ." from the Communion ritual of the Christian mass.

JOURNEY OF THE MAGI

1. The poem is spoken by one of the Magi, or Kings, who visited Bethlehem to see the infant Christ.

SELECTED BIBLIOGRAPHY

WORKS BY T. S. ELIOT

Prufrock and Other Observations, 1917 Poems
Poems, 1920 Poems
The Sacred Wood, 1920 Essays
The Waste Land, 1922 Poem
Sweeney Agonistes, 1924 Play
The Hollow Men, 1925 Poem
For Lancelot Andrewes: Essays on Style and Order, 1928 Essays
Ash-Wednesday, 1930 Poem
The Use of Poetry and the Use of Criticism, 1933 Lectures
After Strange Gods: A Primer of Modern Heresy, 1934 Lectures
Murder in the Cathedral, 1935 Play
Essays Ancient and Modern, 1938 Essays
Family Reunion, 1939 Play
Old Possum's Book of Practical Cats, 1939 Poems

———

Four Quartets, 1944 Poems
      "Burnt Norton" (1935)
      "East Coker" (1940)
      "Dry Salvages" (1941)
      "Little Gidding" (1942)
Notes Toward the Definition of Culture, 1948 Criticism
The Cocktail Party, 1949 Play
The Confidential Clerk, 1953 Play
On Poetry and Poets, 1957 Essays
The Elder Statesman, 1958 Play
To Criticize the Critic, 1965 Essays

COLLECTIONS

The Complete Poetry and Plays. New York: Harcourt, Brace, 1952
The Letters of T. S. Eliot. Volume 1: 1989–1922. Ed. Valerie Eliot. London: Faber, 1988.
Selected Essays. 3rd ed. London: Faber, 1951
The Waste Land: A Facsimile and Transcript of the Original Drafts Including the Annotations of Ezra Pound. Ed. Valerie Eliot. New York: Harcourt, Brace, Jovanovich, 1971.
Poems Written in Early Youth. Farrar, Straus and Giroux, 1967.

BIOGRAPHY AND CRITICISM

Ackroyd, Peter. *T. S. Eliot: A Life*. New York: Simon & Schuster, 1984.
Asher, Kenneth George. *T. S. Eliot and Ideology*. New York: Cambridge University Press, 1995.

Bergonzi, Bernard. *T. S. Eliot*. New York: Collier, 1972.

Blalock, Susan E. *Guide to the Secular Poetry of T. S. Eliot*. New York: G.K. Hall, 1996.

Brooker, Jewel Spears, and Joseph Bentley. *Reading The Waste Land: Modernism and the Limits of Interpretation*. Amherst: University of Massachusetts Press, 1990.

Crawford, Robert. *The Savage and the City in the Work of T. S. Eliot*. Oxford: Clarendon, 1987.

Cuddy, Lois A., and David H. Hirsch, eds. *Critical Essays on T. S. Eliot's The Waste Land*. Boston: G.K. Hall, 1991.

Gish, Nancy K. *The Waste Land: A Poem of Memory and Desire*. Boston: Twayne, 1988.

Gordon, Lyndall. *Eliot's Early Years*. Oxford: Oxford University Press, 1977.

————. *Eliot's New Life*. Oxford: Oxford University Press, 1988.

Kenner, Hugh. *The Invisible Poet: T. S. Eliot*. New York: McDowell, Obolensky, 1959.

————, ed. *T. S. Eliot: A Collection of Critical Essays*. Englewood Cliffs, NJ: Prentice-Hall, 1962.

Litz, A. Walton, ed. *Eliot in His Time: Essays on the Occasion of the Fiftieth Anniversary of The Waste Land*. Princeton, NJ: Princeton University Press, 1973.

Martin, Jay, ed. *A Collection of Critical Essays on "The Waste Land."* Englewood Cliffs, NJ: Prentice-Hall, 1968.

Matthiessen, F. O. *The Achievement of T. S. Eliot: An Essay on the Nature of Poetry*, rev. ed. Oxford: Oxford University Press, 1959.

Menard, Louis. *Discovering Modernism: T. S. Eliot and His Context*. Oxford: Oxford University Press, 1987.

Miller, James E., Jr. *T. S. Eliot's Personal Waste Land: Exorcism of the Demons*. University Park: Pennsylvania State University Press, 1977.

Moody, A. David. *Tracing T. S. Eliot's Spirit: Essays on His*

Poetry and Thought. New York: Cambridge University Press, 1996.

———, ed. *The Cambridge Companion to T. S. Eliot.* New York: Cambridge University Press, 1994.

Pinkney, Tony. *Women in the Poetry of T. S. Eliot: A Psychoanalytic Approach.* London: Macmillan, 1984.

Schwart, Robert L. *Broken Images: A Study of The Waste Land.* Lewisburg, PA: Bucknell University Press, 1988.

Smith, Grover. *T. S. Eliot's Poetry and Plays: A Study in Sources and Meaning.* 2nd ed. Chicago: University of Chicago Press, 1974.

———. *T. S. Eliot and the Use of Memory.* Lewisburg, PA: Bucknell University Press, 1996.

———. *The Waste Land.* Unwin Critical Library. London: Allen & Unwin, 1983.

Sultan, Stanley. *Eliot, Joyce and Company.* Oxford: Oxford University Press, 1987.

Tate, Allen, ed. *T. S. Eliot: The Man and His Work.* New York: Dell, 1966.